How To Cope With The Aftermath Of An Auto Accident

Steps You Should Take If You've Been Injured In A Vehicular Collision In Central Florida

Armando R. Payas

Board Certified Civil Trial Attorney

ISBN: 978-1-941645-94-9

Designed and Published by:
Speakeasy Publications
73-03 Bell Blvd, #10
Oakland Gardens, NY 11364
www.SpeakeasyMarketingInc.com
888-225-8594

DISCLAIMER

This publication is intended to be informational only. No legal advice is being given, and no attorney-client relationship is intended to be created by reading this material. If you are facing legal issues, whether criminal or civil, seek professional legal counsel to get your questions answered.

Payas, Payas & Payas, LLP

www.payaslaw.com

Orlando Office
1018 East Robinson Street
Orlando, Florida 32801
(407) 425-7223

Kissimmee Office
12934 Deertrace Avenue
Orlando, Florida 32837
(407) 847-4071

Deltona Office
1676 Providence Boulevard
Deltona, Florida 32725
(386) 532-7225

TESTIMONIALS

"Armando became my lawyer a few days after I was severely injured because a negligent driver crashed in to me. My first impression was that he was a decent happy man. This gave me confidence because a decent happy man is almost always an excellent professional. At the time we did not even know the extent of my injuries. Armando and his team immediately took charge of my case. Once he took over he encouraged me to rest, heal and recover my life. His approach was from the start, that the main priority was for me to heal and recover my formal life as much as possible. When one is severely injured, the last thing one wants to worry about is the financial consequences of the injury and the legal implications. Meanwhile, his team worked on, contacting all liable parties, the present and future income loss this injury would cause, etc. Armando negotiated with the liable parties and he advised me to be patient and wait until a just settlement was offered. He was more than willing to go to trial if necessary to reach a fair settlement. In the end the liable parties were willing to offer a just settlement. They apparently know Armando and did not want to take their chances in court. Thank you Armando and your team."

- Carl

"I had a case that no one else would take and Payas was able to win my case with minimal effort. They made it easy and very thorough. The service from the front desk was awesome as well!!!! Thank you!!!"

- Samuel

"My girlfriend and I were involved in a very severe auto accident, and were referred to Armando Payas and his firm through family and previous clients. I could not have been steered in a better direction. Armando and his whole team took excellent care of us, providing superb wisdom, communication, and an overall truly sincere care for our wellbeing at all times. Even when I had vented my anger on the attorneys and was being a difficult client, the Payas team still fought diligently to make sure I was properly compensated while still delivering courtesy and professionalism to me as a person and not just a "client". Armando got my compensation to me in a very timely manner and I can truly say I am astounded by the work they put in for me. When it comes to lawyer referrals, there is only one name you should turn to, and that is Payas. You will be in very good hands, their experience and sincerity are top notch."

- Derek

"My wife was in an accident and suffered multiple fractures. After interviewing 5 law firms we chose the Payas firm and Armando Payas. Armando was great to work with and he got us a very good settlement. Throughout the entire process he was very compassionate and professional. The entire staff at the Payas firm was very helpful and caring. We felt like Armando treated us like family rather than clients. If you're looking for a great lawyer, then look no further. Armando is your man."

- Charles

"I hired Payas for my car accident lawsuit and it was a great, smooth and stress free experience. Payas and his staff were in constant communication, very knowledgeable, kind, considerate, and their guidance was accurate for the success of my lawsuit. I would recommend everyone to hire them. If you are involved in a car accident, call Payas, Payas, & Payas. Cases take time and patience, but with this firm you will not worry about their performance and great service."

- Maria

"I want to say a special thank you to Armando and Peter for helping me in my case in a professional way. From day one, Peter took care of every single detail from my case, keeping me updated on every single step of the way. I am relieved that this case is over, but at the same time, I am truly satisfied and will definitely recommend this attorney to anyone who is in my path. I can truly guarantee that they accomplish what they promise. Thank you!"

- Raymond M.

TABLE OF CONTENTS

AUTHOR INTRODUCTION

Attorney Armando R. Payas constitutes the law firm of Payas, Payas & Payas along with his brother and father as the other two partners in the firm. His father was an attorney in Cuba during the Cuban revolution that had actually gone to law school with Fidel Castro. After Castro took the power and determined that he was a communist, attorney Payas' father became a counterrevolutionary leader in Cuba. After the Bay of Pigs they were able to capture the head of the counterrevolutionary movement, who then, through torture revealed the name of the Provencial leaders. Attorney Payas' father was one of the six Provencial leaders. He had to go underground and was able to leave the country through an embassy.

His mother and younger brother Lou were able to reunite with his dad in 1962. After that, his dad completely started all over again. He went back to school, obtained his Masters and his Ph.D. degrees. He became a professor at the University of Central Florida, and chairman of the Foreign Language department. In the 1970s' there were opportunities for Cuban-American lawyers to become attorneys. Attorney Payas' father went back to law school at the University of Florida and received his JD (Juris Doctor) degree, became an attorney after passing the bar in Florida and continued to teach. Attorney Armando Payas graduated from the University of Central Floriday in 1980 Magna Cum laude with a degree in English, Polictical Science and a minor in French. He served as Student Body President and President of the State Council of Student Body Presidents. He graduated law school in 1983 from FSU and was on the moot court team. His brother subsequently went to law school, and in 1992 they formed Payas, Payas & Payas.

The firm is a family law firm, although there are three offices and over twenty-five team members and attorneys that work here. A young partner, Ryan Rudd, has recently been added into our firm. Although Attorney Payas is the managing partner, he does not consider himself the boss. The core values are:

- Integrity in everything we say and do.
- Exceptional service: to provide exceptional service to our clients through attention to one client at a time, and through innovation.
- Respect: To treat everyone with respect, kindness and compassion.
- Growth: We are committed to continuous professional and personal growth.

Integrity, honesty and ethics in all that we do.

Exceptional client service through innovation, continuous quality improvement and total dedication to each client.

Our team members and clients are our most valued asset. We treat everyone with respect, kindness and compassion.

We are committed to continued professional and personal growth.

Those are the core values that form the foundation of this firm. If someone falls short of the values, the firm is always coaching the gap between the behavior and the values. Payas, Payas & Payas is a mission-driven firm and the mission is to help each client get the best possible result in their case. It is also to help them heal through the process. It is to help clients and team members heal so that they can in turn heal the planet in each of their own ways.

When someone joins this firm there are two books that also form the core of the firm. One is called The Four Agreements that everyone must read. The Four Agreements are:

1. To be impeccable with our word. The word impeccable comes from the Latin word Peccable, which means without sin, so to be impeccable with our word is to speak without sin. In other words, not to talk negatively about ourselves or others.

2. The second agreement that everyone in the law firm has to commit to is not to take things personally. Oftentimes when someone is upset, a team member, or a client is going through a hard time and they get upset, it is really not about us. It is someone projecting their issues onto us, and that is their problem. So if we do not take things personally, we do not have to take on someone else's projections, and that

helps us not get our feelings hurt, because oftentimes it is not about us, it is something else they are going through.

3. Do not make assumptions. Oftentimes we make assumptions about everything in life. That is how we are wired as human beings. But instead of making an assumption, and creating a story, just go and find out what the facts and the truths are in each situation. Instead of assuming something, believing it is true, reacting as if it is true, and then, experiencing all the negative feelings that come up around the story, it is better to find out what is really going on so we can respond accordingly.

4. The fourth agreement is to just do the best we can each and every day. Our best varies from day to day. If we are not feeling well, if we are sick, our best is not the same as when we are well rested and ready to go. So we just want to try to do the best that we can every day.

The other book that everyone in the firm must read is called the QBQ, which is The Question Before the Question by John Miller. The book deals with personal responsibility and accountability. Instead of asking questions like why do negative things happens to me. Or why am I not getting the appropriate resources? Change the question to what can I do to change the situation? What can I do to get the resources that I need? It is all about taking personal responsibility for what is going on in our little corner of our experience.

When a client walks through our door, we want to treat them as if they are part of our family. So we want the relationship not to end when the case ends. We want to stay in touch with them and let them know that we are here for them for as long as they need us in the future. So I email many of my prior clients. I stay in touch with them. They will call me to see how I am doing; I will call them to see how they are doing so that they really do form a part of our family. It enriches the experience that we have as attorneys.

The initial interviews with the clients are very important to us because we want to make a connection with them. We want to let them know that we really care about them. It is just not the dollars attached to each case. Since we are aggressive litigators, we work up our cases as if we were going to trial. We know where the pressure points are on cases, and that starts with a very thorough connection with each client. Understanding this is a human process. Their physical pain may be attached to some emotional pain. Although we are not therapists, we try, through the power of listening, to provide a safe environment where they feel that they are heard, and we really understand their stories.

Attorney Payas has been practicing for thirty three years. He is a board certified civil trial attorney. He teaches at Barry Law School as an adjunct professor. He has been recognized as in Thomas Reuter's as a Super Lawyer in 2014, 2015 and 2016 and Florida Legal Elite. He is a member of ABODA, The American Board of Trial Advocates. He talks, lectures and gives speeches to other attorneys. He is a member of the American board of Trial Advocates, the Million Dollar and Mutimillion dollar Advocate Forum. Attorney Payas is very committed to continually improving, to being better, and to delivering a better service for his clients, which he considers as family members.

Understanding The Personal Injury Process

If I am in front of a jury I want the jury to know how much I care about the person that is sitting next to me. The only way to do that is by really understanding them. By walking in their shoes.

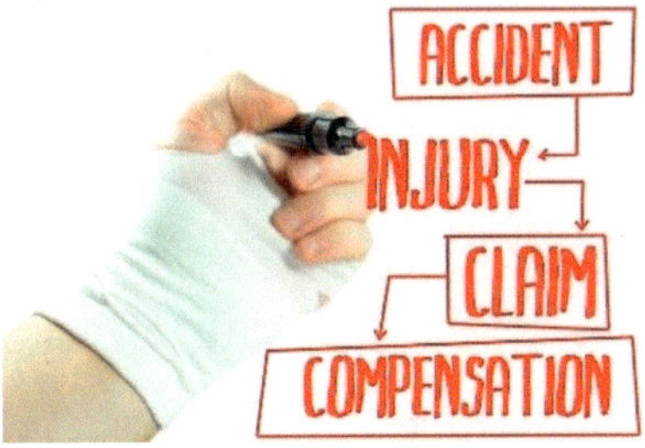

That will sometimes mean going into their homes, getting to a comfort level where we can go to the refrigerator without asking and grab a glass of water if we want. In order to passionately express how an injury has affected someone's life, we want to know as much as we can about that person. As every case is different, it begins with the first interview and doing a good job of understanding the person's background. Having tried a lot of cases, I know where the defense is coming from. We want to head them off at the pass.

For example, we want to know all the prior medical treatment that the client has had and prior worker's comp claims, prior accidents and any prior lawsuits, because we know that the defense is going to say that the injuries are not from this particular accident, but that it came from something in the past. So we head them off. We know that the defense will often say that the property damage is not significant. We want to preserve all the physical evidence from the scene. Photographs of the scene, photographs of all the vehicles involved. Not just the outside of the vehicles, we want to know if there has been a buckling of the frame. So photographs inside the vehicle of the frame, of other damage that can show the nature of the impact. We know they will attack us if the client did not go by ambulance to the hospital right after the accident occurred or if there was a delay in getting to the doctor.

We will try to get an understanding of why they did not go to the hospital or see a doctor right away. If they did then we will express that to the jury, and if they did not we will argue that the person might not have had pain that morning of the accident, but experienced pain later on in the day. It is like a hard workout; you are not going to feel sore muscles that day. You may feel it the next day or the day afterward. So we understand where those pressure points are that the defense wants to use against our client. The next is gap in treatment. The defense will argue that there has been a week's gap, or a four-day gap, or whatever in treatment. By understanding the client we can often tell the jury that this was not the type of person that is in an accident and immediately climbs in an ambulance in an effort to build their case for trial.

They thought they were going to get better, they wanted to get better. Finally when they did not, that is when they sought medical treatment. So it is turning the defense arguments back on themselves. The next argument is that the injury pre-existed the accident. The defense will say there is an injury to the spine that is a degenerative condition or a degenerative change that was already there before the crash. So we work with the best doctors that are here in our community. Whether it be radiologists, neurosurgeons, orthopedics, chiropractors, pain management, rehabilitation doctors, to make sure, the client gets the best possible care and that they get better, because that is extremely important to us, but also that their case becomes more solid.

So the defense may say, "Why did you first go to a chiropractor, why didn't you go to your family practice doctor?" If the client has not gone to a doctor by the time they see us, we will always suggest, go to your family practice doctor first. If you are in a lot of pain get to an urgent care. If they do not have anyone, we will provide them a list of doctors in their area and tell them you choose the one that is most convenient for you. The defense will typically argue oh, you went to that chiropractor because the attorney sent you. So we try to cut that off before they get there.

Another area we are attacked at in trial is family practice doctors.We prepare our clients and say look, when you go to your family practice doctor for a flu shot, and if you are still having neck or back pain, mention it. Because oftentimes, the doctors have these populated records that say no neck pain, no back pain, and it is not true. When you go to the doctors make sure if you are still in pain to mention it to them. So we know where the defense is coming from and we head it off right from the beginning. Another thing that sets us apart is we will ask the client, how do you want to be communicated with? What form? Do you want to receive a text message? Do you want email? Do you want phone calls? Do you want letters? What do you want and how frequently do you want us to be contacting you?

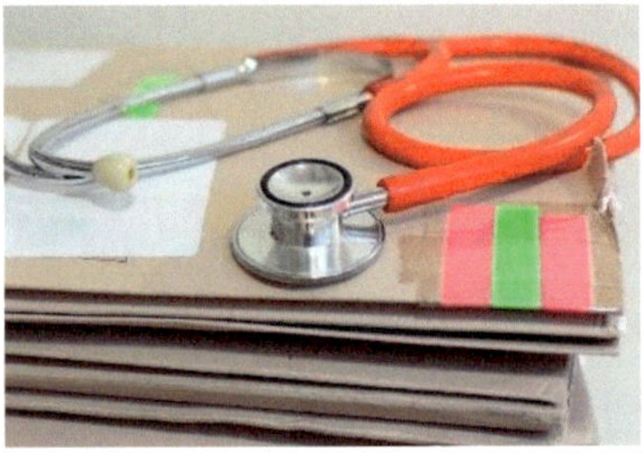

Because not a lot is going on while the patient is being treated in the sense that once we do our initial investigation, send out the initial letters, we have to wait until the patient is done with treatment. But we also want to make sure that they get MRIs if MRIs are requested.

They get to the best orthopedics that they need, and the best MRI facilities. So if there is a herniated disc it will be picked up on the state of the art MRIs, instead of some old machine where the slices are thicker, and will not pick up a herniation or nerve compression. It is a real partnership with our client to make sure they get better, and that they are getting the proper treatment. But we are also building a case at the same time.

When we send our demand we oftentimes send a photograph of the client, a more tailored type of demand instead of a cookie cutter demand. When we go to mediation, most of the time we prepare a PowerPoint with photographs and with the medical records so that we are communicating to the adjustors, we are ready to go, we are not going to leave any stone unturned, and when we go to trial we are going to do the very best we can to win the case. We have come to the conclusion by constantly studying jury selection, through focus groups, through personality testing, that the case is probably won or lost after the jury is selected. It is those six people on the jury that are going to decide what the legal truth is.

We spend a lot of time on jury selection. During jury selection we have an entire team helping us. We are looking at all social medias of each of the prospective jurors;

Facebook, Twitter etc. What party affiliation do they have? What charitable organizations they give to. We want to know as much as we can about the jurors, and we try to add questions that are a little bit different to kind of pinpoint how they are going to react in a jury room. For example, we want to find out if they are a stick to their guns type person or more of a compromisor.

Not that they are always one way or the other, but how would their best friends see them? Are they more talkers or listeners? Not that if they are talkers they talk all the time or if they are a listener, that they do not talk? But how would their best friend describe them? Are they more of a leader or a follower? Not that they do not lead sometimes and do not follow sometimes, but how would their best friend describe them? We ask questions designed to see how jurors will interact with each other and how they will interact in the jury room to give our clients the best possible edge. We ask questions about how they feel about attorneys and the civil justice system and so forth.

I teach jury selection. It is the most important part of the trial. We work very hard on getting our clients the best possible chance at trial through that type of process and through focus groups.

The Most Common Causes Of Auto Accidents In Florida

Florida is unique in that we have so many tourists, particularly in the Orlando area, that are unfamiliar with the roadways. In Florida, we have the afternoon showers so the roadways are slick and wet. But mainly it is the distracted driver. This is

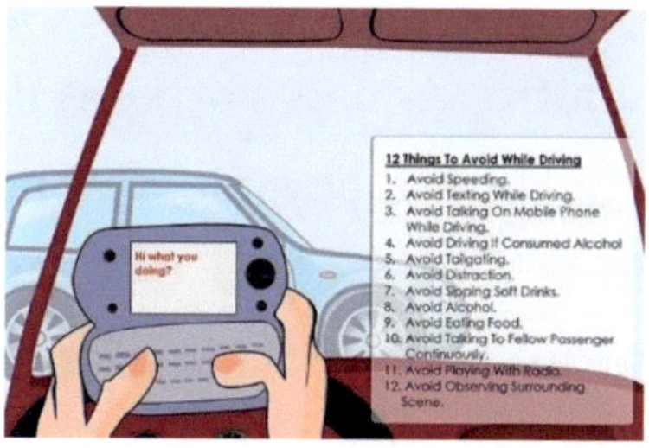

driver that is not just impaired by alcohol or drugs or took an Ambien the night before, but that is on the phone or the driver that is texting. Distracted drivers are probably the major cause of accidents here in Florida. It is very important after an accident to get the cell phone records of the other driver that caused the accident.

We want to know whether they were on the phone texting, or whether they were on a telephone conversation, because if we can establish that, then we can move to amend our complaint and bring an action for punitive damages, and that is something that pressures the insurance companies to tender limits, and depending on the type of injuries it increases the value of our clients' cases. We try to find a punitive damage angle to the case, whether there was an impaired driver through alcohol or drugs, or the more common case a driver that is on a cell phone, or texting. If we can prove that, then the Florida case law allows us to amend our complaint and bring a claim for punitive damages, which then punishes the person for being distracted because that is considered reckless behavior.

The insurance companies are aware of that. An award of punitive damages exposes their insured's personal assets to a judgment, beyond what are just damages to compensate. So it also exposes them to punitive damages which are meant to deter that type of conduct, and that means that a case that might have a limit of $10,000 now might have a value of $100,000, and that forces the insurance companies to try to resolve those cases early on.

Types Of Auto Accident Cases Payas Law Firm Handles

We handle all kinds of cases. It is not just auto. It could be a trucking, motorcycle, bicycle, or pedestrian case. Of course some of the most common are your basic automobile accident cases. Whether it is failure to yield a right-of-way, or a rear-end collision. As well as the trucking or motorcycle cases, or cases involving someone who is struck crossing the street or someone struck on a bicycle. We handle all those types of cases, and commercial type cases too. But in addition we do a lot of medical malpractice. We will handle the larger medical malpractice cases and that helps us with the auto cases, because we have a good understanding of the medicine. Those are the types of cases we see.

STEPS TO TAKE AFTER SOMEONE IS INJURED IN AN AUTO ACCIDENT

If they can get to us early on, then we can really guide them through the process. First, we make sure that they are treated by the best doctors, the best MRI facilities, the best orthopedics and neurosurgeons, people that we would want our own family members or ourselves to go see for treatment. So right after an accident, and the defense will use this against us, but we like to tell our clients, try to preserve the evidence. If there are witnesses jot down their names and addresses because sometimes they will leave before a police officer arrives on the scene, and that has happened many times. The other thing is if they get to us early, we can find out if there are cameras at that particular intersection where the accident occurred.

In Florida there may be independent companies that has access to these videos. They city or county may not have them. So we have to write to those companies right away and figure out, if they have a video of the accident? Because by using the video we can determine who had the green light or who had the red light, or look at how violent the impact was. A picture is worth 1,000 words and if we have video of an accident and can show it to the jury that can makes all the difference. The other thing is sometimes there are business facilities in the area. Wal-Mart, Walgreens, other businesses, and those businesses have cameras.

We will send someone out and talk to all the businesses around and say look, did anybody witness this? But more importantly, do your cameras that show your parking lot also go out to the street and film? Can you preserve that video? With slip and fall cases you want to write to the stores and ask them to preserve video right away, because sometimes they will re-record over it. So you want to do that. If your clients can take pictures of the vehicles at the time that really helps and pictures of the location. Sometimes the accident scene changes, there is construction that happens and the streets are widened, lanes and intersections are altered. So you want to preserve all of that evidence. You want your client to contact their own insurance company just to let them know that they were involved in an accident.

Especially if it is a hit and run, because sometimes these policies say you have a very short amount of time to notify your own insurance company. You want a police officer to be notified and an accident report to be prepared. So preserve all of that evidence for us. Do not talk to the other insurance companies before you have a chance to talk with us because you might say something that hurts your case. We always tell our clients to tell the truth, but it is better to consult with us early on, because we can prevent these pitfalls if we are brought in early in the investigation. We can preserve all that evidence which strengthens the case and either facilitates settlement or increased the value of the case at trial.

If there is not a lot of damage to the vehicle the person cannot have possibly been hurt. We know that is not true, but that is a juror's perception. So we do our best to try to dispel that, although those cases are very difficult to win especially when there is barely any damage to the vehicle. We try to resolve those. We understand that we do not want to risk a client losing the case if we do not have a better than fifty-fifty chance of winning. But that is a complete misconception. There are cases where there is no damage to the vehicle, but then we look under the vehicle and we find some damage and that helps establish that the surgery our client had was necessary because of that accident.

If the person had no prior history of neck or back pain and then immediately began treatment and the herniations look like they are related to the accident you have a better chance of convincing a jury that the accident caused the injuries. You have to do that through good radiologists and medical treating physicians. We need to be able to explain to a jury why a disc looks like it does and that it was recently herniated in this accident. Or if a couple of years have gone by since the initial MRIs and now there are osteophytes, or little arthritic changes we work hard to explain to the jury why the changes are related to the crash. Or if there are degenerative changes in the spine that preexist the crash, how this was aggravated by the crash. But the most dangerous misconception, particularly here in Florida, is that people are just out there to take advantage of the system.

There are so many attorneys that advertise here that jurors come to jury duty and into the jury selection process thinking that victims of accidents just want to get rich. People just want to take advantage of the system. That they are not really hurt. That they are seeing more than one doctor just to build their case. So that attorneys are to blame. They do not trust attorneys. The persuasive advertising is what is driving people to bring more lawsuits in our country. So those are all the misconceptions that oftentimes people in the jury pool have, and we have to work hard to overcome them. The way I do that, is by being as brutally honest as I can with the jury. In other words, not pulling any punches. No sleight of hand. Everything has to be upfront and completely honest. If there is a blemish on our case or a prior accident, anything negative, we are upfront with it and honest. It is also important to remove from the jury pool those jurors with those negative attitudes.

I will tell the jury during jury selection, that what we want from you is brutal honesty and that is what we are going to give back to you. So that when we are going through the trial I want the jury to look at me as the honest guide that is going to help them successfully get through this legal jungle. Even if it means we are wrong on an issue, admitting we are wrong on that issue and being up front about it. So that is really important, because when an attorney stands up in front of a jury, he or she is the least credible person in the entire courtroom because juros think that lawyers, if their mouths are moving they are lying, and that they are not trustworthy, and that they will do or say anything for a buck. We have to dispel all of those misconceptions to get justice for our clients.

ELEMENTS THAT CONSTITUTE A VIABLE AUTO ACCIDENT CLAIM

The best cases are where the liability is clear, like a good rear-end collision with good impact. If there is an element of punitive damages: drinking, drugs, texting, being on the phone, that helps the case resolve. If the person feels injured at the moment of the accident or feels pain and they have to go by ambulance to the hospital, and their complaints of pain at the hospital are consistent with what they then tell the orthopedic doctor or the chiropractor, that makes a better case. If they go to their family practice doctor, and then there is a referral to an orthopedic or a chiropractor, that makes the case stronger. If there is plenty of bodily injury coverage, that makes the case stronger.

If there is not bodily injury coverage but there is, uninsured motorist coverage and there are no pre-existing injuries, then that makes the case stronger. The value of the case goes up if there are no pre-existing injuries or auto accidents, worker's comp claims, prior lawsuits, no history of this person being really a litigious, or someone that is going to file lawsuits over anything. If the person makes a good appearance and can speak the English, that helps. So many of our clients are Hispanic, Vietnamese, or Chinese, and we have to go to trial through translators. That will weaken the case oftentimes.

If there is a need for surgery, that will enhance the value of the case. That will make an insurance company nervous, especially if there is a need for a future surgery or additional surgeries, even though we do not wish that on any of our clients. Generally the higher the medical bills, the more valuable the case. If the injury requires hospitalization, that will help. These factors begin to pressure an insurance company to tender their policy limits, as there is a good chance of a jury verdict above their policy limits. Insurance companies do not want to pay verdicts over their limits.

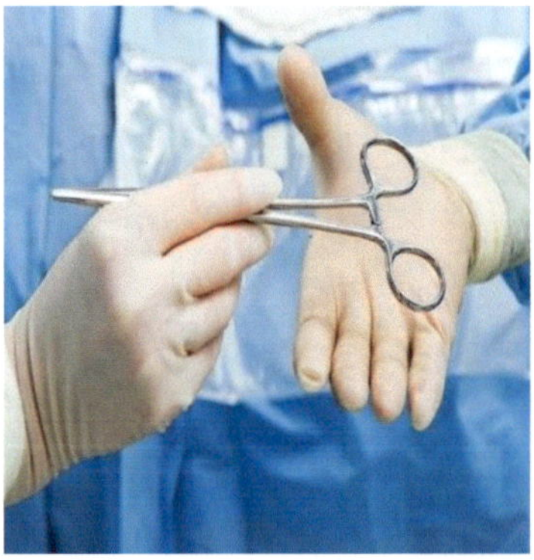

We recently settled a case for $300,000 limits. The medical bills were $125,000 and the person went through surgery. That case only happened maybe a month and a half ago and we were already resolving it very quickly, because the insurance company knew that if we went to trial the jury could give the client half a million or more.

In that case, there was no uninsured motorist coverage, hich really made it difficult for us because the bills were so high. So it is just a whole series of factors that will make a case stronger, if the client makes a good appearance, if they are honest and do not exaggerate. If when asked the question is there anything you cannot do, they say, I can do things, and I want to do things, and I have tried to do things, but now I am limited in doing that. The jury appreciates the candor.

A client that wants to get better wants to go back to work. That helps a lot too. Juries are not sympathetic to someone that just says oh, I was in an accident and I cannot work anymore. That is it, my life is over. Juros do not want to hear that. They want to see that you tried to go back to work, that you tried to go to the gym. That you tried to do things, but maybe now you are limited or you have pain when you engage in those activities. They will be put off by someone that exaggerates their injuries. If you have someone that is truthful, that makes a good appearance, that the jury can relate to, that is honest, that will really strengthen a case.

It is a case by case analysis. Rarely does the perfect case walk through the door where the liability is clear, the property damage is huge, that the client had to be taken to by ambulance to the hospital, received immediate treatment, had no pre-existing injuries, has broken bones, and needs surgery. You know, those cases are easy cases. But, in most cases we have to fight and we have to work with and do the best we can for our clients. We have to navigate prior injuries and pre-existing degenerative disc diseases. All of those different factors that make the cases more complicated or more difficult.

How Do Fault Laws Apply In The State Of Florida?

Florida is one of the few remaining states that have this no fault law. This law was passed in order to provide a person who is in an accident, whether they were responsible for the accident or not, with some basic coverage.

Basic coverage in Florida is $10,000, and it is called personal injury protection. So everybody in Florida has to have it, and what it covers is eighty percent of the medical expenses that the person incurs as a result of the accident, Those medical expenses need to be reasonable, necessary, and customary, and related to the auto crash. It will also cover sixty percent of the person's lost wages, which is proved by getting an affidavit from an employer for the past thirteen weeks with the average salary.

But that is very basic coverage. It does not really cover what is considered pain and suffering and other types of injuries that can come from an auto accident. The trade-off for someone to have that basic no-fault benefit, which is $10,000 in PIP benefits, personal injury protection, is that in order to get other damages like pain and suffering, inconvenience, loss of capacity to enjoy life, mental anguish, you have to prove that the injury sustained in the crash is a permanent injury. That is called crossing the no-fault threshold. That is where oftentimes cases are lost because jurors do not want to award damages for pain and suffering, so they will not find that the person sustained a permanent injury.

We work hard at trial at explaining why the injury is permanent and why the person should be awarded compensation for pain and suffering. Potential jurors oftentimes think, why award someone pain and suffering money when that money does not make the pain and suffering go away? Some people feel that way. We use that line of questioning to try and knock off jurors through what is called challenges for cause when they have that belief, because if they agree

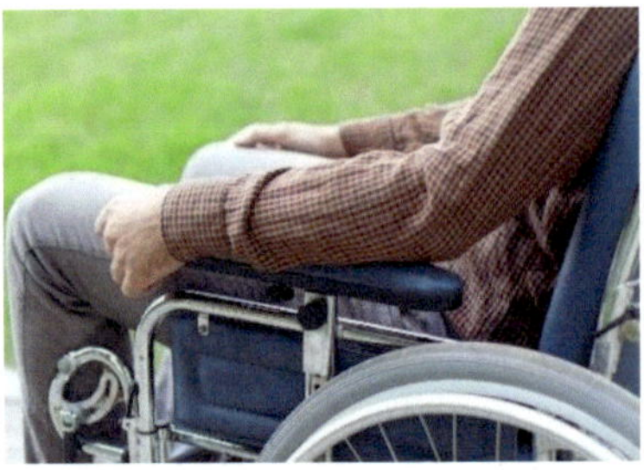

to really follow the law, and if there is a permanent injury, then they need to award those damages. But basically the minimum requirement in the State of Florida is $10,000 personal injury protection, and $10,000 property damage, which just covers the other person's vehicle if they are at fault and 80% of their medical bills and 60% of their lost wages up to 10,000.

That is it. So Florida does not have mandatory bodily injury coverage, and that is coverage that if you run a red light and injure someone, will pay for the other person's injuries. That is why it is extremely important for individuals to buy bodily injury coverage, because that will protect there assets if they are at fault, but also buy uninsured motorist coverage, because uninsured motorist or underinsured motorist coverage is the most valuable coverage you can have on your automobile policy, because that covers you in the likely event that the other person does not have bodily injury coverage since it is not required, or that the other person who caused the accident has less insurance than what you have.

Sometimes they either will not have it, which is forty percent of the drivers on the road, or if they have it, then they only have a $10,000 bodily injury policy, which if you are really hurt badly, that $10,000 is not going to get you very far. That is why you have to have really good uninsured motorist coverage for yourself. Florida requires that if you purchase bodily injury coverage, that your uninsured motorist coverage limits be equal to your bodily injury coverage limits. But then Florida allows you to reject that, by checking a box. What we find is that insurance agents really do not explain the value of uninsured motorist coverage, so they just say sign here, check here, and people end up waiving and rejecting the most valuable coverage available.

They may have $100,000 in bodily injury coverage which is great, protects the other person if they are at fault, but if someone else is at fault, and they cause the accident, and they do not have insurance or have minimal insurance like $10,000 in bodily injury, then they are not going to get compensated for their injuries.

We are one of the few states that are left that have this no fault system in place, and there is a trade-off that in exchange for everybody having to at least have $10,000 in PIP, which available to them whether or not they are at fault, they have to cross the no fault threshold and prove a permanent injury before recovering damages for pain and suffering.

So it is not the best system in place, but at least it provides for everyone with minimal insurance. Now the legislature changed some of that to say that within fourteen days, if you do not seek treatment, go see a doctor, go to an emergency room, an urgent care, and get a doctors report that says that you have an emergency medical condition as a result of the accident your $10,000 in PIP and it is going to be reduced to

> **Personal Injury Protection**
>
> Covers you and your car's passengers
>
> Administered by your own insurance carrier

$2,000. So that is something we try to educate our clients and the public about, and urge them to get to a doctor and get that medical emergency condition report so that they do not get their $10,000 in no fault benefits reduced to 2,000.

WHAT IS COMPARATIVE NEGLIGENCE?

All comparative negligence means is that sometimes both people have some fault in the accident. There are situations where there are no independent witness and one driver says I had the green light and the other driver says no, I had the green light. What do you do in those situations? You present the evidence at trial and the jury is going to decide who they believe or who they do not believe. They will look at the points of impact on the vehicles, who had control of the intersection, and then make a decision. But sometimes they cannot agree on who had the green light or who had the red light. So sometimes they will do apportion fault. They will say it is fifty-fifty. We do not know, so both parties are partially at fault.

There are instances where different witnesses or drivers have different perceptions of what happened, so the jury can always decide one driver is seventy-five percent responsible and the other driver is twenty-five percent responsible, for example. So that is just a concept which allows a jury to apportion fault between the parties. Some states laws provided that if someone was even one percent responsible, it was a complete bar to recovery. In other words, if someone was one percent responsible for doing one little thing wrong, then they can not get anything. But that concept has fallen by the wayside. Now we have comparative negligence and the jury can determine who is at fault and what percentage they are at fault. If the plaintiff, the person who is bringing the action is partially at fault, their recovery is reduced by their percentage of fault.

So if their case is worth $100,000 and the plaintiff is found to be twenty-five percent at fault, then the verdict would be for $75,000. But, Florida has taken it a step further as other states have done as well and if the person who is injured did not have a seatbelt on that is determined to be comparatively negligent as well. In that instance, if they have a cut on their face that would not have happened had they had their seatbelt on, the jury can determine that the use of a seatbelt could have prevented the cut and reduce their damages by twenty-five percent and say that there was some comparative fault compared to the other person who was at fault. So it is really not a bad concept. It does not bar us from getting into the courtroom.

It does not slam the door on us, but it does reduce the plaintiff's damages if they are partially at fault for what happened. In order to discourage drinking and driving the legislature passed a law that says that if a person is in an accident and their blood alcohol is over the .08 legal limit and a jury finds them 51% responsible for the accident, they are completely barred from recovering any damages in their case.

Car Insurance Requirements In Florida

Florida just has a very minimal requirement that does not provide sufficient protection. That is $10,000 in PIP and $10,000 in property damage. The PIP will cover the person who owns the policy up to $10,000, for eighty percent of the medical expenses, sixty percent of the lost wages up to $10,000, and there can be deductibles from there. The property damage just covers the other person's vehicle. If I am at fault for an accident and

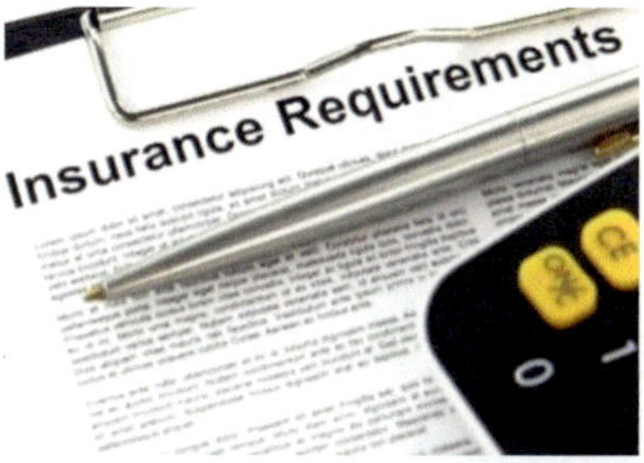

I have the minimal coverage that the law requires me to have and I lose my vehicle that insurance will not cover my vehicle. I needed collision coverage to do that. It only covers my medical expenses at eighty percent up to $10,000, so I am out of pocket the other twenty percent. My lost wage is only covered at sixty percent and that is the combined amount. It never goes above the $10,000.

That is the minimal coverage, which is very little coverage. The important thing to know about personal injury protection coverage is that it goes with you. So if you are struck by a vehicle while you are walking across the street or on a bicycle, your PIP, that $10,000, will go with you, which is good. Everybody thinks they have full coverage even when they have this minimal coverage. But, full coverage means you have good bodily injury limits, which covers the other person. That you have good unisured motorist coverage that covers you if the other person is at fault and you are injured. You have not only the basic PIP, but you can also then pay a little more and get what is called medical payment coverage, which pays one hundred percent of your bills up to that med pay limit whether it be $2,000, $5,000, $10,000, $25,000, $100,000. So you can get your medical bills covered one hundred percent.

You can also purchase collision coverage for your own vehicle if you have a vehicle that has good value and you do not lose your vehicle in a crash. You can always have deductibles there. You could purchase gap coverage if it is a newer vehicle and you have a bank loan, so that if the vehicle has depreciated significantly from the time you bought it you can get the difference between the value of the car at the time of the accident and your loan balance. So that is called gap coverage. You can buy a brand new car and take out a loan for $90,000 and within six months that car is now worth $70,000.

The law says that you only get the value of the car at the moment of the accident, not your loan amount. So your gap insurance will pick up that $20,000 so that you are at least made whole on your vehicle. Then there is uninsured motorist coverage, which is your more important coverage. The interesting thing about uninsured motorist coverage is that it goes with you. If you are in another vehicle and someone crashes into that vehicle and none of the vehicles have bodily injury coverage, your own uninsured motorist coverage will kick in and protect you. If you are walking down the street or on a bicycle and a car hits you and either doesn't have bodily injury coverage or leaves the scene, your uninsured motorist coverage will protect you. Uninsured motorist coverage is critical.

If you have more than one vehicle, if you purchase what is called stacking, you can then put the uninsured motorist coverage on one vehicle on top of the other, and it doubles your coverage, or it triples your coverage if you have more than two vehicles. So we always say get your uninsured motorist coverage at the highest level you can and have it stacked, because that is what is going to afford you more coverage. It can also allow you to stack your uninsured motorist coverage, if you are a passenger in another vehicle, with that driver's uninsured motorist coverage. It provides great coverage and it is not very expensive.

Expected Compensation When Involved In An Accident With An Uninsured Motorist

It is terrible, because if a person who causes an accident does not have enough money to buy bodily injury coverage, then they probably do not have assets. So we are not going to try to take a case to trial and try to win a big verdict and then go after the person who caused the accident because they do not have any assets. We do asset checks through investigators and through different internet programs and software to find out if the person that caused the accident has assets. Do they have homes? Do they have other vehicles? Do they have checking accounts? Brokerage accounts? Stocks? But if a person has assets they are going to have bodily injury coverage for the most part.

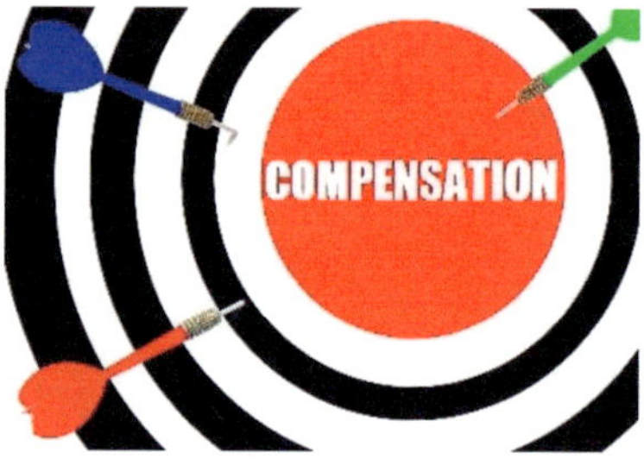

You can sometimes tell by the age of vehicle. If it is a really old vehicle and there is no bodily injury coverage, chances are the person who ownes the vehicle is not going to have many assets. You have about a forty percent chance of getting involved with a driver who does not have bodily injury coverage. So you are really out of luck if you are injured by a driver that falls into that forty percent. That is why uninsured motorist coverage is absolutely critical to have. Insurance agents do not explain it, and the general public does not have knowledge of the importance of that uninsured motorist coverage.

When There Is No Insurance Coverage What Do You Tell Your Clients?

You have to explain to them that they need to do a cost benefit analysis and cut their losses. It is expensive to file a lawsuit, and go through depositions, and bring experts to trial. It can cost $15,000 to $25,000 just in costs. And this doesn't 'include attorney time So do they really want our law firm to spend that much money and time and get a paper judgment which then the person who was at fault can file for bankruptcy, or they will never pay? So we logically walk them through this. We explain, do you really want to spend that type of money? If it were your money, do you really want to spend $20,000 just to teach this person a lesson? Or do you want to go after your own uninsured motorist coverage? Or if you do not have that, then get uninsured motorist coverage and hope that you do not get into another accident.

But, if you do, now you are well protected, and thank God your injuries are not worse than what they are. So it is a matter of performing a cost benefit analysis and cutting the losses. We have had circumstances where the damages were terrible. There was a case where a car broke down late at night. It was dark. The passenger comes out behind the car to push it off the road while his buddy's inside steers the car, and another car comes and rear-ends that vehicle. The poor guy who was pushing loses his legs, and is in the hospital. The medical expenses alone are now $400,000, and he comes in to see me. When we do our investigation, we find out that the vehicle that he was pushing off the road, owned by his friend, did not have any insurance.

The vehicle that crashed into him from behind was driven by an eighteen year-old and did not have any insurance. So there was nothing we could really do for that client under those circumstances. It is really tough. You see death cases where there is no coverage. You see catastrophic injury cases where there is no coverage, and there is just not a whole lot that you can do other than try and help them get their medical bills waived, find public benefits, and go through victim compensation funds if there was a criminal act involved. We try to do that to help them as much as possible. But it is really unfortunate. So that is where people need to be educated. As attorneys we need to do a better job of educating the public. Insurance agents need to do a better job of informing people of the type of coverages they need.

If someone can afford it, an umbrella policy is always good to have too. That is if you only have a $25,000, $50,000 or $100,000 bodily injury policy, for not that much more money you can purchase a half a million or a million umbrella policy. You will want to ask for both a bodily injury and uninsured motorist coverage umbrella Insurance companies do not like to sell uninsured motorist coverage umbrellas, but they are the best coverage money can buy because if there is a catastrophic injury then you can go after your own insurance company for that million-dollar umbrella. Purchase an umbrella policy for both bodily injury and uninsured motorist coverage. That is the best way to protect you and your assets.

Dealing With Insurance Companies After An Auto Accident

Insurance companies will look for ways to deny coverage. So notify your insurance company of the accident right away. Under the contract you signed with them you agreed to notify them of an accident. You also agreed to fully cooperate with them. So if they want a statement from you, you have to give it to them. If they want to talk with you, you have to talk with them. Now you can have an attorney present, and that is highly advisable. So you have to always cooperate with your own insurance company completely because if you do not you run the risk of losing your own coverage, which you do not want to do. Now with the insurance company of the person who caused the accident, you do not necessarily have to cooperate, but oftentimes we will let them know what the injuries are, what the property damage is, because we want to have your car repaired as quickly as possible. Then you have a choice.

Do you want the other side to repair the damage or do you want to go through your own insurance company? If you go through your own insurance company, which is sometimes advisable, you may have a deductible to consider. Sometimes you have to figure out which company is giving you the most value for your car if it is a total loss, or who can do a better job of repairing your car. We help our clients navigate the property damage aspects of their case. A lot of attorneys do not because it is time consuming and they don't get paid for doing this but we understand that the client wants to get this resolved as soon as possible. They want a rental car right away, they want their cars fixed right away. We do not charge any extra legal fees for helping the client get as much as possible for their vehicles. Some of our clients do not speak the language well, so we need to help them get rental cars and help them resolve their property damage. That is an important added value that we give to our clients.

How Should Someone React If Other Party's Insurance Contacts Them?

If they are at fault they may try to get you to settle the case very early on without you having treatment, or without you really knowing the full extent of your damages. They may say, we will offer you $1,000 or here is $1,500 or $2,000, and sometimes people do not realize the extent of their injuries. They do not realize they have a herniated disc and may need surgery later down the road or that they are going to incur medical expenses, need to be on pain medication, need injections or need chiropractic treatment. Sometimes they will try to get you to sign a release for a minimal dollar amount. I have had that happen numerous times in my career where someone will come in and say, the insurance contacted me the day after the accident, they gave me $1,000 and I signed this piece of paper, now I want to sue them.

Well, they just signed a release which means they cannot sue them, in exchange for $1,000. They may have a case that is worth $50,000, $100,000, or more. This is because they do not know the extent of their injuries right after an accident. Sometimes they don't

know the full extent of their injuries until a few days later, or a week, or two weeks or months later. The insurance company may reach out to get a nominal settlement, or they will try to take a recorded statement. At that moment they may be saying well, the only thing that is bothering me is my left knee. Because that is what really hurts the most, and their body is focused on that left knee and is not focused on the fact that they are also having pain in theri neck and their lower back.

Now they play that recording to a jury two years later and they say, you were only complaining of knee pain and now you are also saying your neck and back hurt? So they will use whatever you say to them against you, and that is where an attorney can come in and will guide you through that process and make sure you do not say anything that is going to hurt you down the road. We always want our clients to tell the truth, but an insurance company will not get the entire truth and then that will hurt the case.

What If Your Client Delays Medical Treatment After An Auto Accident?

Do they still have a case? Yes. Has their case diminished in value? It depends on what a jury thinks, and it depends how it is going to be argued. The stronger case is the person that is feeling immediate pain and goes by ambulance to the hospital. At the hospital they do CT scans and it shows there is a broken bone or something really objective, they need treatment right away, and then they have to have surgery, but oftentimes that is not how it plays out. At the moment of the accident the adrenaline is rushing, they are not feeling the pain right at that moment.

So the ambulance shows up and asks are you in any pain, and you say no, because you are not really in any pain at that moment. Do you need to go to the hospital? No, I really do not need to. But then you get home and the adrenaline leaves the body, you go to sleep, and wake up the next morning in pain, or maybe the following day. Two days later the pain becomes persistent. Or the pain begins before you go to bed at night. You wake up and it has increased a little bit, but you still go to work because you have to put food on the table and now the pain's increased a little more but you are thinking it is going to go away, let me just take a little Advil, but it does not go away.

The next day it gets a little worse, and there are tough people out there that say it is going to get better. I am going to wake up feeling better, and they do not. A week goes by. That is still a viable case, and that is how we explain it to the jury. This is not someone that is just going to run to see a doctor. They were hoping their pain would go away. In Florida you need to see a doctor within two weeks and have this emergency medical condition report filed or else your $10,000 in PIP coverage is reduced to $2,000. But we have had cases where the person did not go to the doctor or hospital for a month or three months later and we were still able to get them a recovery. The further you get out the harder it is for us to relate your injuries to the accident.

Sometimes we are still able to, depending on the case and what the medical evidence shows us. Sometimes the person goes and begins to complain right away that they have numbness going into their fingers coming from their neck and they have an MRI and we know it can be a herniated disc. It is compressing on the nerves that run to the index fingers, and we know that is a herniated disc and we can still relate it to the auto accident. So even if the case is weakened by gaps in treatments where a client has treated for a while and then does not see a doctor for months and months, although the defense is going to exploit that at trial, we do our best to explain to the jury that it is normal to have these gaps and it shows that the client is not trying to milk the system.

If there is a bunch of no-shows the defense is going to exploit that. It weakens the case, so it brings down the value. The most important thing is how are six people on the jury going to perceive that? The defense will argue if you are really hurt, then you are going to go in an ambulance to the hospital. We know that is not true, but that can be a perception, so we have to fight against that perception at trial.

Most Important. . .

Importance Of Following Doctor's Advice In A Personal Injury Case

Every time you do not follow a doctor's order the defense attorney or the insurance adjustor on the case, if it is not in litigation, is going to fault your client and argue that they could be better had they followed the doctor's orders. Why did they not get injections when they were suggested? Or if a series of three injections were recommended by the doctor why did they only get one and did not get the additional injections? Why did they not get an MRI if that was recommended? Although usually we do not see that as often, but we see it with injections, people will go for one but not follow up with the rest of that prescribed treatment. The clients do not want to get injections. I understand. It is scary to have a needle go into your back and into a disc, not to mention it is painful. There are a lot of risks associated with these epidural injections.

If the client needs the injections and he gets them and he feels better or feels better for a short period of time and the pain comes back, that will strengthen their case, because these cases have a natural progression. Let me tell you what the progression is and then we will go back to the gaps in treatments and no-shows. The progression is you are either receiving treatment with an orthopedic or a chiropractor. An MRI is done, and that will show there is an injury to the disc or there is not an injury. Then if conservative treatment fails, the orthopedic and physical therapy treatment fails, medications do not work, there comes a point if that all fails, then consider pain management treatment, and if that fails, then we move on and do an EMG. Let us see if the herniated disc is what is causing the numbness.

Let's do a needle EMG, or what we call a nerve conduction and sensory conduction study to confirm nerve damage and if all of that conservative treatment fails, the MRIs are positive, the nerve conduction studies are positive, the needle EMGs are positive, then there may be no other alternative, but to consider surgery. So it has to go through that progression. But if there are gaps in between there, the defense is going to blame the patient. Jurors will consciously and subconciously look for ways to blame the injured party. They will rationalize that if it were me I would do everything the doctor tells me to do. We know that is not true, but they think that way.

I am not going to give this person money unless they did everything they could to get better. So if there was a no-show, believe it, it is going to be a big issue in the courtroom in front of the entire jury, or be put on a big PowerPoint. Look, this person did not show up for this appointment or that appointment. If they were really hurt they would have gone to their appointments. Look, they were offered this, but they are not really hurt if they did not seek treatment as prescribed.

So Jurors are looking for ways to not compensate your client. So you have to figure out and tell your clients, do not ever miss any appointments. You want to get better. We want you to get better. We would much rather you get better than you have a bunch of money, so do everything you can to get better and don't miss any appointments.

Let us follow doctor's instructions. Let us not give the defense more weapons against us that feeds into jurors' attitudes of oh, people are just here for the money. They are just trying to take advantage of the system. They are trying to pull the wool over our eyes. Let us try to really present a truthful case and show the jurors that you wanted to get better and you did everything the doctors said to do because you wanted to get better. That is a much better case than one with a bunch of no-shows.

Importance Of Evidence In An Auto Accident Claim

If you can get, for example, objective before and after witnesses, that will make a big difference in the case. Not just bring a husband or a family member. But if you can bring a supervisor from work that says

this person was a great worker. Here are the employment records. Never missed any time from work and we could always rely on that person. But then after this accident, their performance has since dropped. They started missing time from work. I could tell that they seemed a little bit depressed or that they were in pain. A supervisor, a co-employee, someone like that can make a huge difference in the case.

We do a lot of work in preparing our clients to testify. There is a process called psycho drama where we will sometimes bring in an individual to help the client relive the experiences. That helps us connect more deeply with our clients. We will spend an entire day working on this. In the psycho drama aspect of it, you have a lot of different people in the room that are playing different roles so you are kind of stepping aside and watching the case evolve as it were happening now in real time. So that is a process that we will sometimes use to help us connect more deeply with a client.

In a case we tried recently, had we not spent some time with the client we would not have realized that she lost a child, and that she had lost a mother recently before the trial, and that she was a very prayerful person and had their pictures all the time in her pocket. So she was dealing with that sorrow as well. It is a way of deeply connecting with our clients. But, the evidence is critical. We blow up photographs at trials so that the jury can visually see what is going on. We blow up records, and of course verdict forms. We use the latest technology in the court room such as power points, graphic recreations and animations. It is not just tell me, it is show me. We are such a visual society, and we try to have our experts, which are usually treating physicians, well-prepared and able to get off of the stand and teach the jury why this is a herniation and why this is a permanent injury, and why the medical bills are reasonable, and why the future medical bills are reasonable and necessary, and why the jury should fairly and adequately compensate our client.

That is all a critical part of the trial process. It is not the will to win; it is the will to prepare. The cases are won and lost in preparation, but more importantly, during jury selection.

That is where the cases are really won and lost. You can do a great job and lose the case, and it is because one person on the jury had an agenda, pulled the other five into their way of thinking, and the case is then lost.

How Long Do Personal Injury Claims Typically Take To Resolve?

It really depends. The one we resolved yesterday only happened on February 16th. So it only took four months or so. Others can take years. The one that we went to trial, it was about five years in the making because the client continued to seek treatment and had surgery four years and seven months after the accident. So it just depends on the case. If everything falls into place we can have it resolved within six to eight maybe ten months. If the policy limits are really low and the damages are high, we can resolve them within a week or two. If the policy limits are really high and the injuries are not that great, there is no bad faith pressure that we can bring to bare on the insurance company, and they may want to fight the claim. If the client is not that badly injured and just wants a little bit of money and their medical bills paid, that can be resolved faster.

If the client has significant injuries or thinks they have more significant injuries and they want more money and their expectations are higher, then we have to fight longer. It is really a case by case analysis. Sometimes we resolve cases very quickly, and then for other reasons, if the client is continuing to seek treatment, or there is an issue of liability, this will delay the process. Those cases have to be put into suit. We have to talk to witnesses, and see if we can clarify who was at fault and then try to resolve the case. Cases can be hung up on who is at fault. Maybe the property damage is not that great. There are gaps in treatment. The clients had prior accidents, prior MRIs that showed the same injuries.

Subsequent accidents can happen. There will be an accident one week, and then three or four weeks they will get into another accident. That complicates the case now, because the defense on the first accident will blame it on the second accident. The insurance company on the second accident, will want to blame the injuries on the first accident. It really just depends on the case, and I think the important thing to do there is communicate as best we can with the client and explain to them why the case is taking a little bit longer. As a rule, you cannot resolve a case until you know the full extent of the damages.

You have to wait until the client reaches what we call MMI, maximum medical improvement, where their condition has stabilized. They are not getting better, they are not getting worse, that way we can then project what treatments the patient needs in the future? What is the nature of their injury? Will they need surgery? Will they not need surgery? Once they have reached that point, we know what all the past medical bills are, we can get a handle on what the future medical bills might be, we know if there are lost wages and if so, what they are, and then is there a loss of wages moving forward, and if there is a loss of earning capacity.

Once we have the information to fully and fairly evaluate the case, we do the demand and we try to get it resolved, and we usually give the insurance company twenty to thirty days to review our demand, and then the negotiation process begins. The client always has to be kept in the loop, and give us authority to resolve their case. Although we always try to get the most we can for each client, it is ultimately the client's decision. If they wish to accept a top offer prior to suit, if they do, we resolve the case and negotiate liens. A lot of firms do not do that. We spend a lot of time getting reductions.

We try to be fair with the healthcare provider because they have a business to run, but we are also trying to get as much money in our clients' pockets as possible. If they do not want to accept the top offer, then we sit down and do a very thorough cost benefit analysis, pros and cons analysis. A dollar now is worth more than a dollar after trial, because the costs are not as high.

What Are The Chances Of Winning?

Although it is anyone's guess what a jury will do, we have these certain parameters that we look at. We evaluate the strengths and weaknesses of the case. Then we try to guide the client to the best decision possible for them. But if they want us to go file a lawsuit, we will.

There are pressure points during the lawsuit such as after depositions or mediation where the case can resolve. There are other factors to consider such as what is called a proposal for settlement, which means that if you go to trial and the other side has made you an offer, let us say $100,000 and you reject it, and you only get $50,000 at trial, then since 50,000 is twenty percent less than 100,000 you have to pay the other side's attorney's fees and costs from the time that proposal for settlement expired. It is a double-edged sword. We can do a proposal for settlement at $100,000 and if you win $200,000, since you won an amount that is twenty-five percent more than what you would have agreed to settle the case, then the insurance company or defendant has to pay your attorney's fees and costs.

There are pitfalls involved, and the most important thing is to communicate everything to the client and then help them make the decision that is best for them. That is how we try to move them through the process.

Advice For People Contemplating Self-Representation In Auto Accident Claims

The person will come in and they will go, I have been trying to do this on my own for six months and the insurance company has offered me $3,000, and now I need your help. The problem with that is, the case has now been significantly weakened because they have not received treatments, or they have not had an MRI, or they did not go to a doctor within the fourteen days so they have lost most of their PIP benefits. So I am not going to take a case unless I earn my keep. Unless I really add value to the case. Even on bigger injury cases, we will negotiate with a hospital to bring down bills. Or there is a Medicare or Medicaid lien that has to be reduced, and that can be a big battle. Or there is a worker's comp claim that has to be reduced down.

There are a lot of ways that we will add value to the case where the attorney's fees and whatever our costs are, are going to be much less, and the client is going to end up with much more than had they tried to handle the case by themselves. The insurance companies are in business to make money. They want to pay out the minimum amount they can get away with.. They are not in the business of doing justice, and they are not in the business of fairly or adequately compensating someone. They are responsible to their shareholders and to their bottom line, and so that is their motivation, and they are advocates for their company to pay out the least amount of money possible, and to not pay if possible.

Given that factor on their side, someone that has been injured needs an advocate on their behalf, that is going to get them fairly and adequately compensated, and that is going to fight against the insurance companies and present their case in such a manner that will get fair and adequate compensation. To reduce liens and negotiate with healthcare providers, Medicare and Medicaid, and everybody else, because if hospitals are not taken care of, they can come back and place a lien a home, or they can get a judgment against you. If health insurance companies are not reimbursed through negotiations, they can cancel your health insurance policy and then sue you for not reimbursing them.

There are a lot of pitfalls that we can help the client avoid. The insurance company knows that an individual is not going to be able to successfully try their case and can't afford to bring the necessary experts to trial. So they will try to settle on the cheap and not pay near full value on the claim.

We can make sure that the client is fairly compensated and liens are taken care of and they do not lose their insurance, and doctors are not suing them down the road. And they do not lose Medicare or Medicaid benefits, and avoid collectors calling them at night. It is a way to avoid those pitfalls and it is your best shot, or the injured party's best shot, of getting compensated.

WHAT SETS YOUR FIRM APART IN HANDLING AUTO ACCIDENT CLAIMS?

One of the first things, and attorneys think I am absolutely crazy, is that I give my clients my personal cell number so that they can have access to me. They do not abuse it, most of them. Every

now and then I will get a call on a Sunday night at 11 o'clock for a ridiculous thing that could have waited until Monday morning. But, it is the white glove treatment that we give our clients combined with thirty-three years of experience and, not taking short cuts. We are board certified, which only one percent of attorneys are. We are involved with teaching other attorneys, teaching new attorneys at the law schools. So clients are getting high level individualized care and really exceptional service.

Our case to attorney ratio and to case management ratio is very low. I will have a case manager and an assistant on sixty cases, where these larger law firms that advertise heavily and tend to be mills will have one case manager with over one hundred and twenty-five cases, a part time assistant, and another case manager with the same caseload. We have a full-time case manager and a full-time assistant on only sixty cases. So that means calls are being returned promptly. Emails are being responded to promptly. Investigations are being done completely, and the client is given the attention necessary to maximize the value of their case.

We are talking to doctors and making sure that we are consulting with the appropriate experts. There are few firms that are going to trial more than we are. We are in the trenches going to trial, and the insurance companies know that, so that increases the value of our client's cases. If an attorney that has not been to trial in a while or afraid to go to trial, insurance companies know that, and they will not offer as much money on the case, because they know the attorney's not going to go all the way with it. Another thing we do, is we really work hard at taking down the dishonest insurance company's doctors that come in and testify and say the exact same thing every time.

The person is not hurt, and they could not have been hurt. Or if they were hurt, it was just a minimal strain. It should have only lasted four to six weeks and the person is fine. So we spend a lot of time digging into these experts background, knowing how much money insurance companies pay them. Knowing how often they testify. I mean we know if they falsified or lied on their resumes, if they said they graduated summa cum laude, but they only graduated cum laude, we will find that out and let the jury know. Every little thing that we can find on that expert, we will cross-examine them on and show them to have first, a financial interest in giving these exact same opinions every time, and that they are really not being honest with the jury.

Some of them are very well credentialed. The defense will bring radiologists, orthopedists, neurosurgeons, and the jury can be easily misled if we do not do a really good job at debunking them and showing them and their testimony for what it truly is, which is just, you know, the insurance company trying to save money in saying someone is not hurt. We are guided by our core values and we are really motivated to do the best we can for each client. If you go on AVVO and put my name Armando R. Payas in Orlando and you read what our clients say about us, you will see that what I am telling you is true. You will see that what I am telling you is not just a bunch of talk. That even if the case is worth $10,000 we will go to war just like a million-dollar case and do the best that we can.

That is the level of service we offer our clients. We drill into our entire family and our team members that the client comes first. We want them to experience the white glove treatment. We want calls returned as quickly as possible. We want emails responded to as quickly as possible. We want every client treated with respect kindness and compassion. That is our aspiration. It is an everyday effort to improve and we really try to do the best that we can because we want the relationship to continue, and we honestly do want to treat people the way that we would like to be treated. So that is what we try to do day in and day out. Being on time is the courtesy of kings so, I do not want anyone to wait in the lobby. That is not right.

If there is a 10 o'clock appointment, I want the client to be brought in at 10 o'clock and us to be ready to go. It is not like when you go to a doctor and you have to wait, your time is valuable to us. Everyone has to be treated with the utmost respect and compassion and that starts with meeting our time commitments. The clients have complete access to me and to our teams. I think that is what distinguishes us. We are willing to go that extra mile and willing to make that extra effort to do the best we can for our clients who we really consider family members. That is why the majority of our cases come from our prior clients. I want raving fans when they leave here.

I want them to be busting at the gut to say if you need an attorney; you have to go to this attorney, and let me tell you why. They took great care of me and this is what happened in my case and I am so very happy. Does it happen all the time? No, we are not perfect, but we really make an effort to do the best we can every day to live up to our core values and to help other people.

DISCLAIMER

This publication is intended to be informational only. No legal advice is being given, and no attorney-client relationship is intended to be created by reading this material. If you are facing legal issues, whether criminal or civil, seek professional legal counsel to get your questions answered.

Payas, Payas & Payas, LLP

www.payaslaw.com

Orlando Office
1018 East Robinson Street
Orlando, Florida 32801
(407) 425-7223

Kissimmee Office
12934 Deertrace Avenue
Orlando, Florida 32837
(407) 847-4071

Deltona Office
1676 Providence Boulevard
Deltona, Florida 32725
(386) 532-7225

Made in the USA
Monee, IL
05 November 2026

67386577R00045